l~~y~~g

about

Sleep

2023 Winner
The Laura Boss Narrative Poetry Award
Sponsored by the Laura Boss Poetry Foundation

PREVIOUS BOOKS BY MIRIAM LEVINE

Poetry

Friends Dreaming

To Know We Are Living

The Graves of Delawanna

The Dark Opens
Autumn House Poetry Prize

Saving Daylight

Memoir

Devotion

Novel

In Paterson

Nonfiction

*A Guide to Writers' Homes
in New England*

Forget about Sleep

Miriam Levine

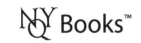

The New York Quarterly Foundation, Inc.
Beacon, New York

NYQ Books™ is an imprint of The New York Quarterly Foundation, Inc.

The New York Quarterly Foundation, Inc.
P. O. Box 470
Beacon, NY 12508

www.nyq.org

First Edition

Set in New Baskerville

Layout and Design by Raymond P. Hammond

Cover photo by John Brook from *A Long the Riverrun*.
    (San Francisco, CA: Scrimshaw Books,1970)

Author Photo © David Lane

Library of Congress Control Number: 2023952456

ISBN: 978-1-63045-111-0

For Julia Markus

and

in memory of

Melissa Shook

and

Jane Davenport Platko

Contents

IV

Part I

Deeper, Darker

Everything bright will darken,
this day, that star, this river,
little frill of blackberry flowers
giving way to insistent fruit,
the boy's voice deeper, darker,
our sky, the swelling cloud,
leaf and the shadow of the leaf,
bird and the bird's cry. It's late.
We're not done with love.

Memory Theater

The shade of my little lamp tints the air
blue and the air fills with a scent like eau-
de-vie and musk. Can't find my shoes. Forget
them. Torn sheet? Forget that. The soft quilt drifts,
my cast-off reading glasses tilt sideways—
slippery sheet, blind glasses, orphan shoes:
a stage for drunken love though I'm sober.
My room—what is it? Waking memory
theater. That April when I wandered
lonely as nothing, it was never those
daffodils that blazed in my brain. It
wasn't men though I flirted with some.
It was me on that dream-silent, fence-bound
street. It was fear like the trembling of joy.

Ben's Rendezvous

On Lucille Place, in Passaic,
I wandered from home,
though forbidden. I was
seven and small for my age.
It was twilight. It was spring.
The trees had come to life.
Their leaves were the light
green of praying mantis wings.
The seeds had wings
that spun them down
to gritty curb strips.
The sound of voices drifted
though open windows like dim
voices in dreams. I went on
past houses with dark halls
that smelled of bleach and wax.
At the corner of Lucille
and Monroe I said to myself,
Go back, go back, yet kept on
past steam-covered windows
of Rice's delicatessen,
past the market on Monroe,
where the grocer with damp
red hands would wring the tops
off carrots, went on till I
reached the corner of Monroe
and Myrtle. It was dark then.
The blue lights of Ben's
were icy and black,
mirror-like panels gleamed
like puddles in the gutter.
I tried to sound out Ren,
Ren like Ben, but vous?

Like goose, I thought. The black
door swung in, and the stink
of sweat streamed out—the smell
of beer, I know now. Beer
and cigarette smoke. It made
me dizzy. Someone laughed,
someone sang, *I'm traveling light . . .*
no one but me and my memories.
I saw people embracing. They
danced chest to chest, thigh
to thigh. The hands did
not move. Oh, they kissed.
The light above the bar was pink,
and the people in command
of their swaying bodies. I
swayed too, drunk on kisses,
my fingers caught on
the skirt of my dress held
by sashes tied at the back,

Memorial School

I see my friends come like sparrows and turn in white light.
Jeanette's collar grazes her neck.
Ann tilts her head so heavy curls un-spiral.
Whispered secret chatter, precious breath, math forgotten,
  books closed.
What did we read? The great ones we'd have years to puzzle
  through.

Always the same street splotched with gold,
always the schoolyard rises at the center
and sinks at the edges in tawny flashes. The grass yields,
a lone gull tips inland, veers and spins the massed clouds
  southward.

And over the greenhouse wooly with dust, puffed clouds gather
  lilac and break from the trees.
I hear Frank gallop, whip his thigh, horse and rider all one.
He whinnies like a horse. The taut invisible reins go slack.
I lean forward and touch the flanks and push back his wet hair.

.

June of Roses

For Nadia Tuéni

With eyes open or closed,
today or tomorrow,
whether night or day,
I can see a horizon's
silver shift back and forth.
I can hear her words,
"O gardener of memory
plant a flower of certitude."
Certain is the memory
of a spider like a crochet
stitch on the pillow edge,
my son's first cry,
my nipple, his mouth,
my ready milk.
Clear is the white sycamore
against sea blue skies,
buds set for spring.
Certain is the scent of June,
June of roses, when I went out
with empty hands, without a purse
or a ticket or a locket,
my socks communion white,
my cotton blouse soft as a flower.

Coat of 1957

In the cold, this
coat,
useless
as silk pajamas
or a tiara,
my trench coat,
creamy as kid.
Rain
pearled on
my shoulders,
the scent
of the lining
the jasmine,
scent of *L'air
du Temps*
tipped
from a bottle
with glass
doves
on the stopper.
Immaculate
coat
into which I
slipped
my virgin body—
worthy, spotless,
diamond
bright,
delta of black hair,
pink
tongue darting
against my teeth
like a fish—
and felt the icy lining

Ah, if I had it now.
Coat
of strong
pockets
into which
I placed my hands
among heavy keys.
Never would I
Iock it into
into that airless
closet shallow as crawl
space, as brides
store wedding
gowns and ask
themselves if
they ever loved anyone.
Pure white coat,
if I had it now
my dog
would place his
paws on my knees,
look at me with his
imploring eyes
and leave smudges
along the worn white seams.

First Lover

No matter how many times I was sure I would
forget him, I see him sitting in an armless
wooden chair, his head above the wooden rail,
the small of his back pressed to the wooden splat,
a foot hooked on the spindle. There's not a fleck
of gray in his hair that shines like hot tar,
not a line in his face white as a church candle
licked by flame. Licked by flame his shocking
pink lips. His was the first body I knew
deeply, more deeply than my parents'.
I wish he were naked and I could see again
the oblique muscles and swelling sex,
but he's dressed in black sweats, waiting
for the race while the voices of other racers
swarm around us, but how will he run
in those polished black leather shoes?
The slippery soles are perfectly new.
He does not make a sound. I grasp
his ankle and ease his foot off the spindle.
His head is turned to the side, angling
toward his shoulder as if he were shy of being
so dead, but I was the one who brought him back
in this form. If this were the promised afterlife
he would appear in his ravishing shape and rise again.

High C

This spring your whole inner life is Little Richard.
You surrender to his octave-jumping high
notes as he shakes out the fringes of his
glittering coat. His boots glitter, too. How
narrow, those feet. And those wigs! How
full. "Is that your hair?" he's asked. "It's
mine. I bought it." Decade by decade,
you see him age but are convinced
he beats back time. And always his
beauty endures. Bare-chested under
his cape, he strolled through Heathrow.
"Man drop his cup of coffee when he see
me. I give him the peace sign." Now he's
streaming through earbuds into your brain,
And you know I'll always be your slave
Until I'm buried, buried in my grave . . .
Your step is easy as you walk south
on Meridian Avenue to your
allotment in the Victory Garden
and the blooming zinnia called
"Zowie," streaked crimson and gold.
You keep time with his time, and the blooms
also seem to sway with the beat.
At night you see him preach about his Jesus;
and you watch his funeral. He believed
he would live forever with Jesus.
You confess you read the auction catalogue
of his things. You don't want his flaming
clothes but you covet his passport,
the photo of him with the impossibly
high pompadour and ink-line moustache,
page after page stamped with seals
of countries he entered and never left.

Sighting

I saw a man on Capital Street
slip from the car he had driven
from a great distant city.
"I'm here," he said, speaking
into his phone and smiling
like those young men
in ancient Greek statues.
His eyes were slanted like theirs
and his hair curled close
to his shapely head.
His arms gleamed, sun struck,
as if he had sailed the bright
Aegean from the island kingdom
of Crete to a small town
where an old woman like me
would say she had seen
a god. I won't go that far but felt
a stinging sweetness fill me
with desire that had no object.

Dancing with George Raft

"At your service, Madame."
His bow, a command.
Dance, his service, so close he seems
to take Lombard from behind. I mean
on screen in see-thru.

The lover I'm good for
dances rumba in clips
I watch in my room
where no one can see me.
In rumba it's all in the hips.

My hair is dry as those lips
below my hips. The muff's like a child's,
just fuzz. There's a tiny lick of heat
fading fast. Like the star I speak
little, cut the bullshit and lift my feet.

"The Charioteer" in Sicily

When I saw a photo of
the statue for the first
time, I was shocked that
anyone could chisel the liquid
shape of a man from such
faceless stone and make stone
cloth drop from chest to ankles in
waterfall folds nearly transparent,
clinging as if wet with sweat.

The right leg thrusts
forward, so weight rests
on the left leg, raising
the hip contrapposto.
The knee's like a giant peony
in bud, the flexed buttocks
horse-like, and the swelling
sex too much for the cloth.

If I were there, I would see
even more closely the snail-curls
at the brow, the seamless
bandeau around his chest.
I would follow the vein
to its source and wonder
at the exhausted, impassive face
as I gazed into another age.

Diamond Head

Where the last snow melted the soil is wet and black
as it was when we first met. Now you're back,
talking, talking, talking. Though you are dead,
you tell me you are surfing at Diamond Head,
riding the wet face of an enormous blue wave.
I see you—hard-muscled, god-like—and hear the wave
collapse in the backwash, your voice, "Cashmere
for me cut to order in Hong Kong. Dear
heart," your voice surges. "A woman taught me
all I know about fucking. I'll show you. See."
My has-been, how I once listened
endlessly to you. My lips glistened
iridescent burnt sienna. We bit
and sucked. I lived in you, eely tongue. It
kills me, your scent, a mix of salty musk and bourbon.
If we had forgiven would we have to go on and on?

Daffodils

The spring day when after the dark subway
the light was blinding and the last of the snow
melted, trickling into the gutters, but still
there was the scent of winter—
icy, evergreen, alpine, flint.
Work was finally over and there
were flowers like lit candles
on the corner near Old South Church
and just enough money for daffodils
that came dripping from the bucket,
daffodils carried home to our room,
where we sat without talking,
and I became part of the sun-struck
halo, the snow-washed high windows,
the silvery mirror, voices rising
from the street, walls saturated
with ghost music, passengers peering
from train windows and those arriving
to vanish in the distant Back Bay streets.

Part II

Two Widows in Summer: Late Afternoon

All of the sunlight came burning to reach them
through whitened branches of sycamore leaves.
Where a streak broke in, the leaves weakened it.
Where the old women rested was half dark
spiced with the odor of sycamore bark.
They had no eyes for the tree sheltering them.
What they loved was their unhurried time.
What they did together always was talk.
Who was born. Who still lived. Who died.
Who fell. Which children did well. Which did not.
Quick to mock lying politicians, they kept
mockery brief to save breath that would run out
as their eyes had run out of tears. There's no use
complaining, they agreed, but knew each other's
complaints, as intimate with those as they were
with summer dresses their needles had pierced.
Their feet hardly worried the ground.
When slow dusk came on, erasing the day,
when they were finally done with talking,
they did not give themselves to the fireflies'
flickering light or the darkening grass
or the dampening ground or the small branch
or the few still green early fallen leaves.

Blue of Provence

The day is brighter than gold. You think
of nothing as you walk, one step then
another, lindens fringed with fresh green,
yesterday's rain in the gutters, buds
of roses ready for June. And now
you doubt yourself; you don't know why
you're alive while your friends are dying.
The sky is cloudless; the breeze drops veils
on your shoulders and shelters you. Forget
your unimportance. The sky is the blue
of Provence. Your every breath is life.

Elegy for a School

The greenhouse windows green
with algae, shelves damp with moss,
the cool corridors half-tiled
and the black-rimmed clocks
in Roman numerals. Shattered
are the classrooms' high
yellow windows with window
poles I used to imagine would
propel me down the Grand Canal.
The flash cards are scattered, books
rotted; broken, the oak panels
of the library, as all will be
broken, silent the young voices,
the brave and the timorous,
burnt and scattered, laid down deep,
gravestone, a hard page.
Birds are in good voice, fluty, high.
When one stops, another begins.

Forget about Sleep

The little deaths between breaths—
Mim, be afraid. Tremble. Here's
yesterday, your brother
broken, blue-eyed. Always
your brother. And your mother
who sang in the dark—
will the next breath come? Where
is the pink-lipped doll
of childhood, soft blanket,
the street below, the one
tree and cinder-strewn curb strip,
those sparrows, the smell
of rain, tiny windows
of the black screens where blue rain drops
swelled, your crib, the fever
and the cool hand? Where is
your first friend,
who in your dreams danced
through walls, her deep-hemmed
cotton dress, the pocket too small
for her hand? Where is her dog,
those eyes cunning with love?
Be afraid of the falling ash
staining the maple, the room
of the future with nothing in it. Go
ahead, worry. Mim, do you hear
me? Your hands remember their
claws no matter how much
you cut the nails and slick
on polish. Or do they?
Mim, forget about your
self. The radiators are too hot
to touch, wind thrums

down the vent. There's thunder.
Not enough air for the candle.
Forget about sleep. Mim, why would
you ever want to leave the earth?

Don't Go

For Stephen

I dreamed you called me on the phone and drawled my name.
"Where are you?" I shouted. "Right at your door, dear Mim."

And you were! In the long black coat of your youth,
when we read Hart Crane and drank ourselves awake.

"Don't go," I called, reaching out, but you broke,
and fibers made tracks like iron filings drawn by a magnet.

There were punch holes in the sky. My eyes stung.
"Think of yourself," you would say, kindest of all our friends.

Appreciator, shy of great deeds, you preferred praise for little thir
your narrow feet, the coat's flirting with shoes, the price of Zinfar

Cardinal

Still in your nightgown, bare
feet on the cool grass, white
hair like floss: I watch
you open the sack and pour
sunflower seeds onto the tray
for any cardinal like me you
believe carries the soul of your
dead darling come to protect you.
Some say we're angels,
other insist our sudden flash
means a lover—a voice,
a searing kiss. I don't envy
this black oak tree locked
to a twenty-foot taproot.
I flit and rise, in seconds
measure your loneliness, your need.
Yours is a human dream. How can
your kind believe there is
a soul in me—feathered, red, pure?

Last Sight

When I leaned over my dying father,
his hospital gown gaped, and I saw
his sex now small as a child's, violet
and palely veined, the thin legs once
muscled and strong, the withered thighs.
My heart stuttered. With a shaking hand
he covered himself. I gave him my vain
bright smile. Leaning closer, my face
over his, I thought, How stylish I must
look in my new rakish hat. His eyes
flickered then glowed, held me, held
me in his smiling unbearable gaze.

The Story of Daphne

Not even a god can
catch her, fast as he is,
Phoebus Apollo, the Shining One.
It's clear he will rape her.

She prays to her father,
and he, a river god,
turns her into a laurel tree
just as Apollo overtakes her.

His breath is hot on her neck.
Her skin hardens. Still
he presses his lips against the bark,
feels her beating heart.

She cannot feel him,
only water rising from a hidden stream.
Each spring she comes back
impervious, intact, flowers borne
in pairs beside a leaf.

Apollo consoles himself.
Laurel wood will make his lyre,
leaves wreathe his head,
tree like a flag at the door of Augustus.

There are fathers like Daphne's
who trap daughters they
mean to save, and daughters
like Daphne who are numb to human touch
yet green and fragrant.

Kitchen Death Wish

Heat from the cellar boiler scorches
the floor. My mother's stockings
coil around her ankles like bumpers.
She licks the tip of her index finger
and pushes up the page of the paper.
The corner falls over the story.
Tight scrolls of the window shades
crowd the frame, the pulls dangle
in the breeze from the window
open to the damp smell of cinders;
on the clothesline, white flags
of our pillowcases, night creases,
night odors, night stains scrubbed out.
My hair is white, my mother's dark,
richly curled at the back of her neck.
She sits so lightly on the edge
of her chair and touches the back
of my hand—I can't stand the touch,
ghost hand light as a fruit fly's,
creeping, unsure, papery, though she
tries to comfort me and, as always,
fails. "Sit with me a while," she says,
but I stay upright. She lifts a page,
lets it drop, smooths the fallen paper:
"Such terrible things in this world."
I put my hand on her shoulder, making
sure my touch is not too light, not too
heavy. Dutiful, false. "You've come,"
she says. Her bones are so small.
How did she ever give birth to me?
I am tired of her. I want never to have
been a daughter, never to have been
born into this cindery world. I want to stop,
kneel, give up and let runners pass by.

Aunt Jen Speaks from the Afterlife

My birthday! And not a word,
not a thought, not a dream from you.
Though you wear my ring, though the three
diamonds shine, though you of all people
know I was more than the shy-seeming person
who hesitated in doorways while the rooms
were crowded with our drunken family.
You saw me in my Astrakhan coat,
and voguish black hat. You loved to hear
the story of the shimmy skirt of white
fringe, nothing but fringe skimming my knees
when I danced. The dead know me for my
style and reserve. "She's thinking her own
thoughts," they say when I turn away from
stories of warriors no matter how brave.
Better to serve Aphrodite with her doves
and black cherries. Remember the dish
I held out to you heaped with cherries,
the winters when entranced you watched
me rub the tip of my pinky across
the lipstick nub and with that fingertip paint
my lips? I'd kiss the top of your head, cup
the soft nape of your neck. To shorten your skirt,
I would kneel and pin up the hem while step
by step you turned. There are seasons here,
a light dusting of snow like sugar, never a storm.
When you come, drink from memory's stream not
from Lethe's no matter how much they urge you.

Posing

In the last year of her life, once the tumor was cut
from her brain, and she had a little more time,
Melissa and I posed for photos. There we are
looking normal, each with a dog on a leash,
the dogs quiet at our feet, also seeming to pose.

When I took her to lunch, she left her head bare;
black stitches punctured her scalp; her hair
was gone, and there was a seam near the once
definite hairline now only fuzz. With the tip
of her tongue she licked the corner of her mouth
and smiled at our server whose lips trembled.

She's sly as a cat up to mischief, I thought,
as she had been in her acclaimed self-
portraits with all of her aging body naked.
"I may be able to eat something," she said quietly.
My glance slid away, and when I looked back
into her eyes I talked about nothing, bright nothing.

Watching Birds

They flit low in early morning across School Street
past the half-way house for released convicts

as a lone car strains up the steep hill
toward Monadnock in the blue distance.

And now another car, electric, soundless,
empty except for the obscured driver.

The clear, clean light and scent of lilacs
make the fast-disappearing birds so

piercing now. Another friend is dead!
He who was supposed to outlive us all.

I think of the verve and flash of robins
Dickinson watched from the edge of her garden,

breathing in the spice of lilacs while the morning
sun found a cold space in her and filled it.

History

My God, it's a pigsty,
this compound—I don't
know what to call it.
I don't know the man
mowing paths through yards
of August burnt-sienna grass.
His house is a trailer,
stove in, broke in,
a tin-can hovel
on a road in Maine.
And there's a bus!
Sunk to the sills.
Drowned chassis,
busted gunnels,
empty wheel wells
caught in ragweed—no,
goldenrod and bracken.
The roof's thin now—
beetle back, beetle shape,
dome yellow as tansies.

There's a skiff, too,
on lichen, on rocks,
up there, dry to the keel.
Bilge gray, stranded—
hull, shell, wreck.
And higher still, a house
desolate, abandoned.
There's no cash to fix
the Greek revival.
Blown windows float
in that upper story.
I see straight through to
sky, mussel-shell blue.

How does the man
live in this mess?
How do I with mine?
Our years stack up.
History—the failures.
I like to think he may
not see them anymore.
And what he remembers?
How can I know?
There's too much ledge
to bury his people here.
On Cemetery Road,
sandstone marks
the graves, takes water,
lists, sinks, flakes.
Pale orange from
iron in the stone
obscures the dates.
The names dissolve.

Our Frailty

Glow so bright the high clouds are sun-like.
And those rays like the sun's corona.

Out and out and out, the low clouds stretch.
The shirred wing-sweep breaks.

The wisps are no match for the moon's
smoky halo, sulfur-green.

Gorgeous colors wheel far above us.
We're dimming silver, like figures I once saw

on the back of an ancient mirror tarnished like dusk.
Still they embrace in the oxidized haze—sky, sea, couch?

I'm not sure. Still they are young, breath-born, unlike us.
The dusk is fragrant but not with pity for our frailty.

Oh silver-clouded air.

Lighten Up

Listen, Mim, be a featherweight.
Sure, you once admired Susan Sontag,
who called herself a "zealot of seriousness."
It "nourished" her, she insisted.
And those heavy texts in French and Czech.
Seldom the work of light-hearted writers.
She didn't smile or suffer fools,
hardly ever slept, kept going on speed,
never took a nap. Not me. Not now.
Go ahead, Mim, be frivolous, spend
an hour choosing a dress. Fish out
that necklace you haven't worn for years,
the one from your friend Jane
with the figure of Venus, born from
the frothy sea. She loves
mirrors. There you go—lipstick
cherry-red, toe nails lacquered pink.
When that fool of a critic thinks he's brilliant,
offer a bemused smile he takes for approval.
Sip from a glass of cold champagne
and take yourself home to your
zero-gravity La Fuma chair and read
Jean Rhys: *It's funny how well you*
can remember when you lie in the dark
with your arm over your forehead.
Two eyes open inside your head . . . .
The road goes along by the sea.
The coconut palms lean crookedly
down to the water. (Francine says that if
if you wash you face in coconut-water
every day you are young and unwrinkled
no matter how long you live.)

Opening More

Gray-blue sky and fog,
grayer still, hung
between land spits:
there was no horizon, all air,
and black dot of the buoy,
and blue opening more.

West—a long pink slit
in big-scaled billows,
which, as minute by
minute passed, turned
fruity, darker, lit like wine
held to fire. West again,

the lighthouse signaled
green beyond the jetty.
Water came in low, the harbor
tilted or was it land? The sky
went out and in the fade
four yellow torches blazed from the pier.

By the Water

There's no trace of the tide or the marks of the waves,
wave after wave erased, the horizon dissolving.

Ours were the low-ceilinged room and red-hot fire
subsiding to blue, collapsing to ash.

Tide mark of memory, you won't bring back bleached wood,
chill windows and the stinging smell of clam flats.

How we laughed at little nothings and slept through the night,
when now I wake in the dark and turn on the light to read:

*A cloud, small, serene, floated across the moon. In that moment
of darkness the sea sounded deep, troubled. The cloud
sailed away, and the sound of the sea as a vague murmur,
as though it waked out of a dark dream. All was still.*

At the End

At the end of summer when nights turn cold
he'd sleep alone in the small downstairs room
with the low window open so he would hear
the crickets' throb and feel the dark roll over the sill.
The wind sent a leafy branch against the clapboards.
Beyond the black oaks the moon rose and his heart
beat to the rhythm of the crickets that seemed never to end.

Compline

2 AM, the moon has set, and the evening star,
our balcony umbrella folded in pleats like a scarf,
faint voices from the street and John sleeping

while a pacemaker keeps his heart beating
fifty-two times a minute. OK says
the little screen on the white-faced device.

It's time to pull the drapes across the rod
to shut out the glare of lights streaming
from the roof of the police-station garage,

time to lock the door, turn off the lights,
slip into bed next to John
and hear him breathe and sleep at last.

What Will I Need?

When I tilt back in the zero-gravity chair, my pen is charged
with green ink, my book open like a cat on its back.

I search for words I knew by heart. I want to mark them.
"The thing is to have made someone care," writes Henry James

but then print wiggles, swims and blurs. Where are my glasses?
Seeming miles away in the room down the hall.

What will I need when I'm dying? Grace to speak a tender wor
strength to touch my darling, softness to let go of everything.

Part III

Exclusion

It's a relief to drift past lovely things that exclude me.
It would take a machete to open hedges of flaming xora,
a bolt cutter to reach jasmine, blindness to miss red flags,
though the ocean looks open, smoky blue, and gorgeous;
and vanity to intrude on neighbors, who stand face to face
near the door of our building, blessedly unaware of me,
one speaking, the other stricken with sympathy.

Waiting for the Light to Change

For Trish

Zebra longwings rising,
white jasmine in bloom,
the street oddly quiet,
and I remember my friend
describing how she waited
to cross a street near the great
cathedral of a northern city
where Mass had just ended,
while on the opposite side
a woman also waited, praying
the rosary, my friend guesses
because the woman gazed
into air as if she had come
from Mass wanting prayer
to go on and on and on,
her fingers sliding from bead
to bead in the pocket of her coat,
my friend was certain. It must
have been spring since thin
snow had just melted,
and the coat was navy blue
and the scarf yellow—her hair
covered in yellow—those colors
usually worn together in spring,
and remembering my friend
I feel less alone as I walk
among strangers through
the lightest web of possibility
that I too may be seen clearly
without knowing when
or if it happens.

After the Big Rain

After the big rain a small one sprinkles from palm trees.
Everything by the sea is a flower; beach umbrellas
are umbels of wild carrot; white sails are petals;
blasted tulips, the wind-buffeted gulls; pansy-faced, the children;
fallen flowers, the sunbathers; fluttering, the leafy sarong.
But Kamani trees on Meridian escape likeness.
They cool us in fragrant shade. They have their own flowers.
The buds open, they burgeon, small, white, immeasurable.
They have their own incomparable leaves.

Ash Wednesday

Lent is the time of year
when women appear
on Fridays at twilight
with gladiolas in tight

bunches with every bud
closed. It's difficult to know
the color unless you get close
enough to see a flush of yellow,

or paper-cut scarlet.
Down Euclid, down Meridian,
stems propped against necks,
blunt ends in their palms,

they come, each with heavy stalks,
two huge bunches. What do they do
with so many? Put them on altars,
I imagine. By Sunday they'll bloom

up from the bottom like fire
set at the base of a stake—
churches are named for saints.
Women who walk home tired

after hours and hours of work,
on Wednesday will be stained
with ashes. I wish they wore
flowers, ruffled ones, and the plain

rose giving out the odor of grace—
the ancients wore garlands
woven from roses and dill.
Though the Graces—foolish to say it—

preferred those who wreathed their hair
with flowers, I send them my prayers,
as if now those beneficent Graces
could ease the gladiolas's heavy weight.

Flowers

My double wears a scarf like mine
in shades of red falling on her breasts
and rising in flashes when wind catches the fabric.

My double is writing in her blue notebook.
Is she writing "Sciuri," the name of this café
where "little anodynes. . .deaden suffering"?
She's sipping from a cup she's rubbed on the rim

with lemon peel. Between strokes of her pen
the pen tilts back, the holding fingers relax,
and she starts again, her unsmiling aspect
gathering around a serious thought; like mine,

her cane hooked on the back of her chair—
like stage props, these white chairs.
I am writing in my notebook about sick people
and yesterday's sunlight and how it came

down on the girl unconscious in the grass,
lit up her shriveled boots, her open hand,
the string bracelet that some call Friendship,
darkening briefly under a passing gull, shone

again on the street, on the drugged boy
jammed between snake plants in a stone box,
glazed his golden tanned legs, unable,
though it warmed them, to hide their frailty.

My double is writing. Does she notice
the urn at Sciuri from which cactus stalks put out
green paddles with thorns in patches
and red flowers crowding the edges?

Is her heart beating fast from strong coffee?
Is she saying again that she must change her life?
Does she forget herself as I do when at
Sciuri I remember the word means flowers?

In the Park

Because you see the laurel grove, you notice shadow filling space
    under branches so the grove becomes your brief oasis.

Because you look beyond laurels, you see other trees dropping f
    from branches still wreathed in pink.
Blossoms on the grass in windrows tell you what the wind does.

Thin as a whip, someone is sitting cross-legged, staring like murc
    into a hand-held mirror.
With pointed tweezers she digs at her eyebrows.
Like a machine, she plucks, wincing at the sting, as you have do
Though you remember prophetic Whitman saying of creation, "
    this I swallow, it tastes good," you tremble with pity and do not swa

Someone is sleeping upright with cloth draped like a prayer sha
    over his head.
Between damped-down edges a profile trace appears.
Though his jeans are so heavy with dirt they look like metal han
    to his legs, his leg stirs.
Because you hear laurels speaking beyond speech, you hear the
    sleeper, "God, I told you, I told you . . . believe me, God, I told

You cannot enfold any of them.

Oh shadow without substance.
The tree trunks are moist on one side in a wavering line the sun
    not yet reach.

Pigeons at the Condo

Though some say kill them, the words you love
are shadow, twilight, flood. They come with mist
and drift in dreamlike states that free other words,
like wave, ocean, wing—a conspiracy.
In whispers. Know thyself, the ancients say,

and you obey, hearing words as breath
laurels breathe. When wind releases a leaf
you are released from the insistent
throaty call of pigeons turning and turning
in a balcony dance among excrement.

CDs you string on long strings from the rail,
swing, flash, twirl. Light as they are,
they knock when wind drives them.
Light as they are, they shock and terrify.
Where pigeons once turned there's only a flash.

Night at Admiral Towers

When our three rooms are quiet and the Cowway
Air Mega signals clean with a circle of blue light,
and the building is silent as silver locked in a drawer;
and silent too the dum-dum bass that beat through walls
of the condo next door, whose owner flashes his card
impresario@gmail.com, and elevators wait at the starred
floor like dark empty buses, and there's not even the whoosh
of traffic or a plane's roar, but only a glass door and still
palmettos, Venus rising in the east, and pink
neon-lit pilasters that flank the entrance
to Flamingo Plaza where lithe polo players once stayed,
who are now in their graves, and with feet near the threshold,
a little cloud from my breath on the clear sky of the glass,
I give in, give in to the quiet streaming inside me.

At the Victory Garden on Collins Avenue

When I'm among flowers—these
zinnias of super-saturated red,
untarnished gold cosmos,
the pentas and tit-waver
Emilia coccinea so scarlet—
I swear they save me as they
save the monarch, the gulf
fritillary and zebra longwing
of dazzling black chevrons,
brushing, brushing, brushing
the fuzzy hearts of pollen,
and there's hope I might become
merciful and just when I place
myself in such a way that no
shadow falls on the flower,
no darkness on those wings beating
in rhythm, seeming to fly
but poised on a bloom.

Small Hotels

These seaside hotels with women's names
take the surf's roar without answering back.

The Patricia, The Barbara, The Julia:
I'd try them in turn, one for each year, south

for the season at last at the Julia.
The elevator would have room for only

me and one suitcase. The windows could be
opened. There'd be no wake-up call.

At twilight my room would fill with pale blue,
morning light coat the walls like a Rothko.

The pages of my notebook would swell from humid air
but still take the mark of the pen's inky ball.

There would be a little desk, and, in the shallow drawer,
stationary printed with a crest and the hotel's name.

At night, in lamplight, I'd write to friends,
words light as kisses on a newborn's face.

Already Here

What I might have wished for is already here,
the long loose line of pelicans flying north that seems to break
    but comes together,
the man on the sidewalk near 6th Street, always the unlit cigar
    in his hand guarding a promise,
the trans swishing through Flamingo Park, shaking out her curls,
    calling, Darling, Darling, Darling, I'm here,
beautiful boys racing the spongy track, backs shining with sweat,
wave after wave filming the sand with amethyst,
colors fading, the waves always and always returning,
the flash of green parrots flocking, the egret balancing on the top
    of the hedge,
odor of cedar, the negligent filmy curtain dragging on the sill,
casino ships on the horizon with no destination,
the old woman who asks for directions to Alton Road
    and my correct answer,
the young man who suddenly appears and says, I'm going your way.

Part IV

On Foot, No Smart Phone: Finding My Way in a New Town

Coordinates should be perfect, but mine drift
in skies pink as sunrise, the fading sky,
one long goodbye at sunset. A driver
lifts his stunned face and rocks to heavy
metal that blasts through shut car windows.
Someone's running in the far distance—
streets like science fiction scenes after every
human's vanished. Is this the way? Or this?

Stone-curbed streets turn their backs on the river.
Floodlights flash on a dome of gold—this must
be the city's center. That massive building's
a vault in which the state buries secrets—wherever
I am I don't belong there! A voice like the voice
of a muse sings in my head—spire, bridal wreath, lilac—and these
three appear at the last turn toward home as if sent by spirits.

No One Has To

No one has to command the rose
to stain the air with knock-out red.
No one has to tell clover to take bees
to its heart. Don't pray for Fleabane
or Black-Eyed Susans to flower. They
will not come when they are called.

No one has to coax Pearly Everlasting
or prime Smooth Aster. Don't bow
to flagrant plants shamelessly seeding
themselves: Goldenrod, Tansy, Touch
Me Not, Rag Weed, Thistle, Rough
Blazing Star: like gods, they do not need us.

Geranium

When frost was certain,
I heaved a pot
of geranium up
by the rim, pushed
it into the house, lifted it
onto the bottom step,
then to each higher step.
The pot was too heavy
to carry without stopping
for a breath. I reached
the second floor and shoved
it to a southwest window.
Poor thing left to languish?
No! Fifteen months inside
and it's blooming against cold
glass, the flower-head made
of smaller flowers, starry red
explosions, scalloped leaves
fed on nitrate, phosphate, potash
in sludge ground from fish parts.
The stems seem indifferent
to gravity. And the buds, too.
They cluster and swell
on spindles. Rub a leaf
against the nap—that scent
lemon-red and slightly
oily . . . I won't move it. Some
plants prefer an inside room,
a high ceiling for a sky.
They don't miss the stars.
I'd never put them on
a grave. Cut flowers

are better there, a bolt
of color like sudden
memory, but one cold night
and all the colors dull.
Stones are even better.
Headstones and smaller
stones, those pebbles
left to show someone came.

Union Street

The calm fall night when blazing leaves were invisible
and the curtain of the living room window
blurred the gold dome of the capitol building
recognizable though beautifully veiled;
and three windows of the house on Centre Street
also came through but these in pale blue;
and I thought everything is in its place—
hushed and muted, even the street.
There was enough light in the room to see
the rug's edge and the arm of your chair;
I did not have to do anything but rest.
The door to your bedroom was open,
and your nightlight showed a familiar path
I might have taken to watch you dreaming.

The Watcher

On the porch at the broad face of the house
where light gathers but barely broaches the window
John watches for hummingbirds
while I stand in his room out of his sight.
The newspaper lies blurred in his lap.
Old as he is the weight of years seems
light as a passing breeze. He leans
toward the red sun-struck feeder filled
with syrup and goes on watching,
noiseless, patient, disarmed.

I remember seeing our young son like this
when he kneeled by the bay window
and gazed at the pale new leaves of the maples,
keeping himself utterly still,
as if to invite the blue sky to drop
to his shoulders and shelter him.

Now at the corner of the porch
a flash of ruby from the Ruby Throat,
a blur of wings, needle-like beak
probing the sweet opening,
back and forth, then gone.
The air still trembles, there are traces.

Darling, in waiting, the self forgets itself.
Into that poised still attention
something lovely may come.

Early Snow

Summer heat and long bright days are gone,
summer when the couple across the street
would come out in their bathrobes and sit
reading on the balcony and I would watch
the quiet spectacle and wonder, Had they
showered after making love, the fever
of fucking gone for such compatibility?
And though it's October there are suddenly
red Christmas lights blazing in their windows—
too early, too early, but what do I know! This
morning there's snow shivery as drifts at the creche.

On the Way to the Food Coop

When I walk by the State House
into Capitol Plaza, sound shuts
off as if someone has thrown
a switch, and I'm stuck in the dead
air of my vision: There is no one
here—not a soul or a dog or a bird.
Doubling off, I see myself from afar:
a small lone figure in outline;
the outline a live wire. It jolts
my brain; my scalp tightens.
Is this what mad people feel? I don't
know but think the world we've made
is really cold and weird, no pine
or laurel here, but a colossal flag
collapsed on a pole, brick mortared
to brick, the self-important dome, bronze
statues of generals raised high on pedestals,
stalled scabbards, blunt boots, stuck mouths
sealed in metal. And I think of Blake's
"mind-forged manacles" and freeze
by the statues then lift my feet and walk
on, remembering— eggs, bread, milk—
and hear my cart creak and feel it jump the cracks.

Why Should I Be afraid?

Scarlet Runner,
I love you. Your
hoods of cochineal,
your flashy blooms
that spread wings,
drop keels, triple leaves
at the axes and green vines
that shoot skyward and wind
overhead tough as iron wire.

The fuzzy knife-shaped pods
dangle and swell in the cold.
Oh those fat autumn seeds
the size of thumb knuckles,
each seed in a hollow
like an eye under a shut lid,
each primed for the future.
They sprout and go as far as
they can through dirt and oceans of air.

November

These days when wind wears itself out and sun warms the side
bare-throat days, when white floss bulges from milkweed pods
but does not blow away, and leaves float like scattered thought
when the hinge between fall and winter does not move,
and those nights, too, when long past midnight, windows
are flooded with light, and it seems everyone on this street is a
tuned to something we cannot see, something I imagine faith

Undertow

When the winter sky was
azure and mild as May,
my friend talked cheerfully
about her son at school
in London, her eyes
staring
and wide open.

Her pale hands
were about to touch—

about to touch, I thought,
in prayer

and did not move.

Do You Dare?

It snows on the leaf, on the branch on the rose,
on marigolds, shriveled as they are.

It snows on the threshold, on the window, snow clumped like cotto
Snow drifts on the street, on the road, deep on the curb strips,

greenish whirlpools of snow under the streetlights,
white on the dome of the Greek Church across the way.

It snows on the gravestones, on the evil and the good.
In the garden, on the statue, the Buddha's lips sealed in ice.

And cracks between flagstones obliterated, the ground all one thii
Do you dare call it unity, cold grace, white communion, blessed sil

Then wind carves the drifts so at the foundation of the house
there's snowless space and a white crest like the crest of a wave.

Covid Times

Some people do good in the world, but I'd rather haunt windows
  with a view of the church
to imagine long tapers melting under flames that vanish like
  "flesh swallowed by spirit."

"Pray for this state," says Saint John the Righteous, whose words
  live on the church's website.
"Ask for a body light as smoke. Pray till you are nothing but soul"—
  not for me, not for me:

I love bodily things. Shadows softer, light paler, cutting wind erased:
the city anticipating spring—that ice-glazed shrub like a fountain
  frozen in air,

even the fogged glasses of the masked young priest,
the swelling of witch hazel and the willows' flush.

Candle to the Flame

For Jim

Clear skies when in the east the moon is clean as ice,
I would think that's where the sun will rise: east and east

again sunlight floods our room, the tables blaze, the unnecessa
candle leaves the smell of smoke, a trace on the candle stick.

"Why are we here?" my friend once asked. "Our species . . ."
"To read each other's poems," I laughed. In his there are

crows, swallows, swifts, doves, red-winged blackbirds
ancient seers would see as auguries and I dare to see as hope,

but aren't we also here to sacrifice the candle to the flame and
   see light fade?

That Winter

That winter when the night sky was violet, I was sure I would
   remember it,
and the sight of unbroken snow in the morning, I would remember
   that too,
and the cat waiting on the step to be let in,
and on clear nights the evening star just over the hemlocks,
and the tree in the young couple's window lit long after Christmas.
I was sure I would remember those starry white lights,
and the couple's windows and tree going dark at their bedtime,
while I read by the light of a single lamp.

Unshed Tears and the Snow

When I hear great Callas sing
Nell'ora del dolor,
In my hour of sorrow,
heat breaks the dam in my chest
and tears seem to well but don't
come no matter how much they
tease at the back of my throat.
Then later at the window,
the curtain pushed aside,
I see the street turned white,
and the trees and roofs, and path.
As I kept longing for tears,
snow fell from a windless sky
and night came on with no sound.

You Ask Yourself

Near that house with the green door, you ask yourself,
What would it be like to be a different person,
contented to cook a meal and mend a tear
and live in that house and not be driven?

You think it may be time to leave your old self,
not like the Carmelites who take a vow of silence,
a new name and pray day and night for the world,
but something like them, someone who speaks less.

Raga

Let me imagine we come again
to the great hall to hear the master.
We're all ages and purged of regret.
We do not think of the past or lust
for food or worry about our looks.
The master plays on, notes falling
like a shower of seeds, the summer
a distinct season once again. Wild
fires have stopped burning, seas recede,
the precious sky at last an infinite blue.

Envoi

My little paper boat, my book,
sail though the world in the wake
of Sappho, the great one
you will never overtake.
Float on the brimming stream,
reach an open hand, spill your secrets,
stain the palm, show virtue and sin,
the breathless kiss of syllables,
an intimacy that in life did not exist.

ACKNOWLEDGEMENTS

Thanks to the editors of the following periodicals in which these poems have been published, sometimes in different versions.

American Writers Review: "You Ask Yourself," "Raga," "At the End"
Apple Valley Review: "Ben's Rendezvous," "Deeper, Darker"
Coal Hill Review: "Daffodils," "Memory Theater"
The Glacier: "Kitchen Death Wish"
Ibbetson Street Review: "The Watcher"
Lily Poetry Review: "Diamond Head"
Northern New England Review: "Candle to the Flame," "Geranium"
On the Seawall: "Do You Dare?" "Exclusion," "Union Street," "In the Park," "That Winter," "Unshed Tears and the Snow"
One: "Forget about Sleep"
One Art: "Pigeons at the Condo," "November"
One Hand Pointing: "Undertow"
Plume: "Dancing with George Raft"
Red Letter: "'The Charioteer' in Sicily," "Watching Birds"
Threepenny Review: "High C"
Valparaiso Poetry Review: "Two Widows in Summer: Late Afternoon"

"Union Street" was republished in *Poetry and Places.*

Gratitude for their support of these poems to John Lane, George Kalogeris, Julia Markus and José Antonio Rodríguez. Alan Feldman offered superb editorial advice.

Thanks to the Laura Boss Foundation for all their help and for sponsoring the Laura Boss Narrative Poetry Award.

Appreciation to Thomas Adams for educating me about John Brook and photographer Gary Samson for reproducing the cover photo. Both are founders of The John Brook Archive which generously granted permission to use the cover photo.

For expert editing, a bow to Wyn Cooper. Thanks also to all at NYQ Books, especially Raymond Hammond.

My cousin Francesca Liechenstein was a sensitive reader of many of these poems and helped me get certain facts right.

NOTES

"High C." Little Richard, Richard Wayne Penniman, 1932-2020; singer, musician, composer, originator of Rock and Roll.

"Dancing with George Raft." Carol Lombard (1908-1942) actor; George Raft (1901-1980), actor, dancer.

"Posing." The friend is Melissa Shook.

"Lighten Up." Voyage in the Dark. New York: Norton Paperback, 2020, p. 153.

"By the Water." The passage in italics is from "At the Bay" by Katherine Mansfield.

About the Author

Miriam Levine is the author of five previous collections of poetry, a memoir and a novel. Her work has appeared in *American Poetry Review, The Kenyon Review, The Paris Review, Ploughshares, The Southern Review,* among many other places. She is a fellow of the NEA, a grantee of the Massachusetts Artists Foundation, and a recipient of a Pushcart Prize. Her work was supported by stays at various artist's colonies, including Hawthornden Castle, Yaddo, and Ledig House, where her residency was funded by the Diane Cleaver Fellowship. Born in Paterson, New Jersey, Levine left her home state for New England, where she earned degrees in Comparative Literature from Boston University and a PhD in British Literature from Tufts University. At Framingham State University in Massachusetts she was a professor and chair of the English Department and coordinator of the Arts and Humanities Program. She was the first Poet Laureate of Arlington, Massachusetts. Levine lives in Florida and New Hampshire with her husband John Lane.

Printed in the USA
CPSIA information can be obtained
at www.ICGtesting.com
JSHW081549140224
57313JS00002B/61